Dinosaurs

Also edited by Lee Bennett Hopkins

Dinosaurs

POEMS SELECTED BY LEE BENNETT HOPKINS

Illustrated by Murray Tinkelman

VOYAGER BOOKS/HARCOURT BRACE & COMPANY

SAN DIEGO   NEW YORK   LONDON

Requests for permission to make copies of any part of
the work should be mailed to: Permissions Department,
Harcourt Brace & Company, 6277 Sea Harbor Drive, Orlando,
Florida 32887-6777.

The illustrations on pages 25 and 27 are redrawn from paint-
ings by Charles Knight, courtesy of the Department of Library
Services, American Museum of Natural History.

LIBRARY OF CONGRESS CATALOGING-IN-PUBLICATION DATA
Dinosaurs.
Includes index.
"Voyager Books."
SUMMARY: A collection of eighteen poems about dinosaurs, by
authors including Lee Bennett Hopkins, Lilian Moore, and
Myra Cohn Livingston.
1. Dinosaurs—Poetry.   2. Children's poetry, American.
[1. Dinosaurs—Poetry.   2. American poetry—Collections.]
I. Hopkins, Lee Bennett. II. Tinkelman, Murray, ill.
PS595.E93D48   1987   811'.008'036   86-14818
ISBN 0-15-223495-0
ISBN 0-15-223496-9 (pb)

G F E D
Designed by Barbara DuPree Knowles
Printed by South China Printing Company, Hong Kong

Every effort has been made to trace the ownership of all copyrighted material and to secure the necessary permissions to
reprint these selections. In the event of any question arising as
to the use of any material, the editor and publisher, while ex-
pressing regret for any inadvertent error, will be happy to
make the necessary correction in future printings.
    Thanks are due to the following for permission to reprint the
copyrighted materials listed below:

ATHENEUM PUBLISHERS, INC., for "When Dinosaurs Ruled the
Earth" from The Apple Vendor's Fair by Patricia Hubbell.
Copyright © 1963 by Patricia Hubbell; "Fossils" from
Something New Begins by Lilian Moore. Copyright © 1982 by
Lilian Moore. Both reprinted with permission of Atheneum
Publishers, Inc., an imprint of Macmillan Publishing
Company.
CURTIS BROWN, LTD., for "The Museum Door" by Lee Bennett
Hopkins. Copyright © 1973 by Lee Bennett Hopkins. Reprinted
with the permission of Curtis Brown, Ltd.
FARRAR, STRAUS & GIROUX, INC., for "Dinosaurs" from More
Small Poems by Valerie Worth. Copyright © 1976 by Valerie
Worth. Reprinted with the permission of Farrar, Straus &
Giroux, Inc.
LILLIAN M. FISHER for "Dreamscape," "I'm Glad I'm Living
Now, Not Then!" and "To Brontosaurus—A Gentle Giant
Dinosaur." Used by permission of the author, who controls all
rights.

ISABEL JOSHLIN GLASER for "How the End Might Have Been" and
"What If . . ." Used by permission of the author, who controls
all rights.
FRAN HARAWAY for "Prehistoric Morning." Used by permission
of the author, who controls all rights.
HARCOURT BRACE & COMPANY, for the text of the last page of
Whatever Happened to the Dinosaurs? by Bernard Most.
Copyright © 1984 by Bernard Most. Reprinted with the per-
mission of Harcourt Brace & Company.
MARGARET HILLERT for "Dinosaur." Used by permission of the
author, who controls all rights.
BOBBI KATZ for "Unfortunately." Used by permission of the
author, who controls all rights.
SANDRA LIATSOS for "Plant-Eater." Used by permission of the
author, who controls all rights.
DAVID MCKAY COMPANY, INC., for "Lines on a Small Potato" from
Poems Made Up to Take Out by Margaret Fishback. Copyright
© 1973 by Margaret Fishback Antolini. Reprinted with the
permission of the David McKay Company, Inc.
MARIAN REINER for "Dinosaurs" from The Way Things Are and
Other Poems by Myra Cohn Livingston. Copyright © 1974 by
Myra Cohn Livingston; "To the Skeleton of a Dinosaur in the
Museum" by Lilian Moore. Copyright © 1979 by Lilian Moore.
All rights reserved. Both reprinted by permission of Marian
Reiner for the authors.
VICTORIA DAY NAJJAR for "The Last Dinosaur." Used by permis-
sion of the author, who controls all rights.

For Anna Bier—a gentle giant of the publishing industry

Contents

Introduction

Sixty-five million years ago, dinosaurs disappeared from the earth. Though there are dozens of theories that have attempted to explain what happened, no one really knows. Their disappearance, however, has certainly done nothing to diminish their popularity. They continue to fascinate people the world over.

In this book, you will meet poets who have sung the praises of these mighty creatures who once roamed the earth and whose bones now grace museum halls.

Let your imagination soar as you enjoy this excursion into a bygone era.

Lee Bennett Hopkins
SCARBOROUGH, NEW YORK

Dinosaurs

The Museum Door

LEE BENNETT HOPKINS

What's behind the museum door?

    Ancient necklaces,
    African art,
    The armor of knights,
    A peasant cart;

    Priceless old coins,
    A king's ancient throne,
    Mummies in linen,
    And a dinosaur bone.

Fossils

LILIAN MOORE

Older than
books,
than scrolls,

older
than the first
tales told

or the
first words
spoken

are the stories

in forests that
turned to
stone

in ice walls
that trapped the
mammoth

in the long
bones of
dinosaurs—

the fossil
stories that begin
Once upon a time

When Dinosaurs Ruled the Earth

PATRICIA HUBBELL

Brontosaurus, diplodocus, gentle
  trachodon,
Dabbled in the muds of time,
Once upon, upon.

Tyrannosaurus raised his head
And rolled his evil eye,
Bared his long and yellow teeth
And bid his neighbors 'bye.
His pygmy brain was slow to grasp
The happenings of the day,
And so he roamed and slew his friends
And ate without delay.

Brontosaurus, diplodocus, gentle
  trachodon,
Dabbled in the muds of time,
Once upon, upon.

Allosaurus awed his foe,
He awed his friends who passed,
His teeth were made for tearing flesh,
His teeth were made to gnash.
Taller than a building now,
Taller than a tree,
He roamed about the swamp-filled world
And ate his company.

Brontosaurus, diplodocus, gentle
  trachodon,
Dabbled in the muds of time,
Once upon, upon.

Eaters of their friends and foe
Or dabblers in the slime,
Their pygmy brains were slow to grasp,
Once upon a time.

Dinosaurs

VALERIE WORTH

Dinosaurs
Do not count,
Because
They are all
Dead:

None of us
Saw them, dogs
Do not even
Know that
They were there—

But they
Still walk
About heavily
In everybody's
Head.

What If . . .
ISABEL JOSHLIN GLASER

What if . . .
    You opened a book
    About dinosaurs
And one stumbled out
And another and another
    And more and more pour
Until the whole place
Is bumbling and rumbling
And groaning and moaning
    And snoring and roaring
And dinosauring?

What if . . .
    You tried to push them
    Back inside
But they kept tromping
Off the pages instead?
    Would you close the covers?

I'm Glad I'm Living Now, Not Then!

LILLIAN M. FISHER

When earth was yet a little child
Dinosaurs lived free and wild.
Some as big as spacious homes,
Some as small as tiny gnomes.
A few had wings to fly the skies
With giant beaks and searching eyes.
Harboring murder in their breasts,
They stole the fledglings from their nests.
One giant breed lived deep within
Dark waters with its kindly kin.
Still others wandered mean and bold
And ate each other, I've been told.
I know what might or must have been—
I'm glad I'm living now, not then!

Prehistoric Morning

FRAN HARAWAY

Ponderous, he wanders by the lake;
Swaying among ferns, he stops to take
Mouthfuls of new shoots. Contented, he—
Dragging massiveness—expectantly
Plunges his enormity into
Cooling waters, disappears from view.

Plant-Eater

SANDRA LIATSOS

Brontosaurus, thunder lizard,
great Jurassic dinosaur
dined on topmost leaves and branches
of tall prehistoric trees.
He walked upon all fours with ease
and never strayed from water's edge,
for when an enemy drew near
he slid away from plants and sedge
into the watery depths to hide.
He feared meat-eaters who could slide
their teeth inside his soft weak skin.
His mouth was weak. He couldn't win
a fight with any carnisaur.
He wanted a peaceful, gentle life
with lots of plants and not much more.

Dreamscape

LILLIAN M. FISHER

A giant came into my dream
And thundered to and fro.
As thunder-lizards often do
He traveled high and low.
He shook the hills and mountaintops
And spilled the seven seas.
He drank eleven rivers,
He ate a hundred trees.
But even thunder-giants sleep—
He wandered off to find his bed.
I didn't notice where he went,
I simply, quickly, woke instead!

The Last Dinosaur

VICTORIA DAY NAJJAR

The last dinosaur
Lays his head down,
Tired at last,
Tired from the long journey.
No food here, no warmth,
Only earth, shivering and cold,
So different from the past.
Rocky formations spring everywhere
And palm fronds no longer sway.
Gone are the balmy days,
For cold has come,
Bringing blue death for so many
Prodigious creatures now fallen
Who once roamed earth, cousins
Of this last dinosaur
Who now waits for death,
Sighs, closes his armored eyelids,
Lays down his spiked limbs.

Gone is the need for weaponry;
For who is left to do battle?
All have perished
As will this, last Dinosaur.

How the End Might Have Been

ISABEL JOSHLIN GLASER

The tall ferns shivered
And the palm trees quivered.
A single bird call
Wiffled the jungle air,
Its long chill note
Hanging as if frozen there.
Then a glacier came
Slip-sliding through,
And the forest got so cold
    The lips of all
The dinosaurs turned basic blue.
    It was the end.

       Good-bye.

          Farewell.

             Adieu!

Dinosaur

MARGARET HILLERT

The dinosaur,
The dinosaur,
Was once
But isn't
Anymore.

If it were,
You must agree,
Then you
And I
Just wouldn't be.

I confess
It's much more pleasant
To know
That he's
The one who isn't.

To Brontosaurus—A Gentle Giant Dinosaur

LILLIAN M. FISHER

Gentle giant dinosaur,
Slow moving, kindly herbivore—
Unprotected, no defense,
With tiny head, the rest immense.
You walked about on stumpy legs
And laid your ancient, giant eggs
In brush and grass at water's edge,
So babes could feed on plants and sedge
And swim to hide from carnivores
Who fiercely screamed upon the shores.
Did terror strike your reptile heart
When threatened to be torn apart
By tooth and horn and saber scales?
Your kind could only fight with tails.
But tails have never won a war,
My gentle giant dinosaur.
Yet science knows a simple truth—
The horn, the claw and saber tooth
Have also vanished from our earth.
New species have been given birth.
Museum rooms now house your bones
Alongside footprints sealed in stones.
Your ghosts are gathered from afar,
My gentle giant dinosaur.

Dinosaurs

MYRA COHN LIVINGSTON

Their feet, planted into tar,
drew them down,
back to the core of birth,
and all they are
is found in earth,
recovered, bone by bone,
rising again, like stone
skeletons, naked, white,
to live again, staring,
head holes glaring,
towering, proud, tall,
in some museum hall.

To the Skeleton of a Dinosaur in the Museum

LILIAN MOORE

Hey there, Brontosaurus!
You were here so long before us
Your deeds can never bore us.
How *were* the good old days?

Did you really like to graze?
Did you often munch
With a prehistoric crunch
On a giant tree—or two—or three
For lunch?

As you went yon and hither
Were you ever in a dither
When your head and distant tail
Went different ways?

Did you shake the earth like thunder
With your roars and groans?
I wonder. . . . Say it's hard
To have a conversation
With your bones.

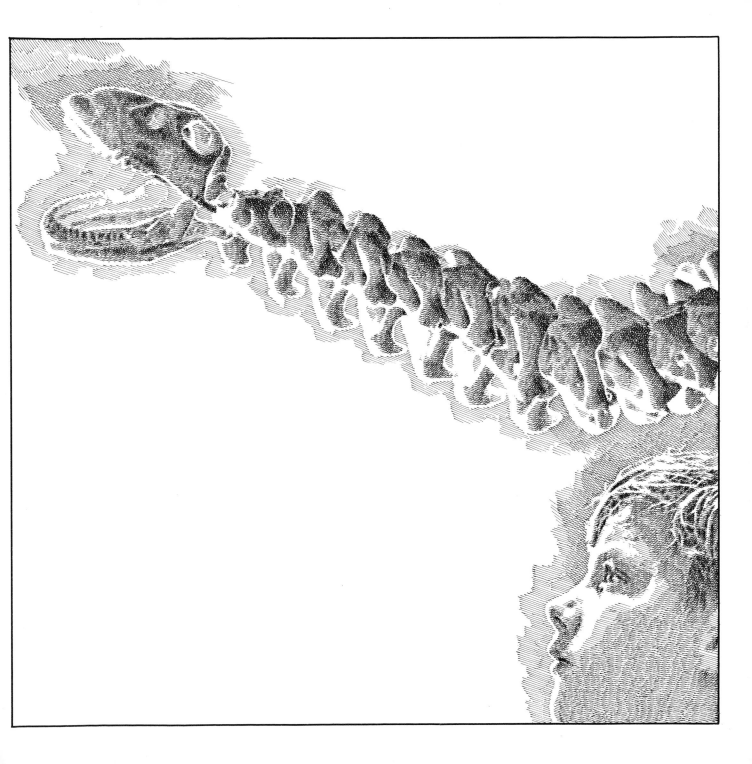

Unfortunately
BOBBI KATZ

Dinosaurs lived so long ago
they never had a chance to know
how many kids would love to get
a dinosaur to be their pet!

Lines on a Small Potato
MARGARET FISHBACK

Reflect upon the dinosaur,
A giant that exists no more.
Though brawny when he was alive,
He didn't manage to survive,
Whereas the unimpressive flea
Continues healthy as can be;
So do not whimper that you're small—
Be happy that you're here at all.

FROM

Whatever Happened to the Dinosaurs?

BERNARD MOST

Whatever happened to the Allosaurus,
the Brachiosaurus, the Camptosaurus,
the Ceratosaurus, the Cetiosaurus,
the Coelophysis, the Corythosaurus,
the Dimetrodon, the Diplodocus,
the Hypselosaurus, the Iguanodon,
the Megalosaurus, the Monoclonius,
the Ornithomimus, the Parasaurolophus,
the Plateosaurus, the Plesiosaurus,
the Protoceratops, the Scelidosaurus,
the Stegosaurus, the Trachodon,
the Triceratops, and the Tyrannosaurus?

Do you know?

Index

OF AUTHORS,
TITLES, AND
FIRST LINES